WITHDRAWN

ESCAPE!

THE HACKER'S HIDEOUT

SOLVE YOUR WAY OUT!

ACCESS DENIED!

Use your TECHNOLOGY skills to ESCAPE!

Kevin Wood

 Gareth Stevens
PUBLISHING

Please visit our website, www.garethstevens.com. For a free color catalog of all our high-quality books, call toll free 1-800-542-2595 or fax 1-877-542-2596.

Cataloging-in-Publication Data
Names: Wood, Kevin.
Title: The hacker's hideout: solve your way out! / Kevin Wood.
Description: New York : Gareth Stevens, 2023. | Series: Escape!
Identifiers: ISBN 9781538277294 (pbk.) | ISBN 9781538277317 (library bound) | ISBN 9781538277300 (6 pack) | ISBN 9781538277324 (ebook)
Subjects: LCSH: Puzzles--Juvenile literature. | Problem solving--Juvenile literature. | Logic puzzles--Juvenile literature. | Technology--Juvenile literature.
Classification: LCC GV1493.W663 2023 | DDC 793.73--dc23

Produced for Gareth Stevens Publishing by Alix Wood Books
Designed and Illustrated by Alix Wood
Interactive website created by Kevin Wood Software
Editor: Eloise Macgregor

Printed in the United States of America

CPSIA compliance information: Batch # CSGS23 For further information contact Gareth Stevens, New York, New York at 1-800-542-2595.

Driving home from school, your dad says he needs to pick up some files. He parks in the underground office parking lot and tells you to wait in the car. He says he'll only be two minutes. After twenty minutes, you're bored. You get out of the car and look around. Maybe you should go through that big metal door and call for him?

That was a mistake! The heavy metal door locks shut behind you! This doesn't look like your dad's office either. You must have come through the wrong door. All you can see is one long shadowy corridor. You can see some lights at the other end. Maybe you can get back out that way?

HOW TO ESCAPE!

Use your technology knowledge to puzzle your way out of the hacker's hideout. Solve puzzles to get the codes you need to open a series of locked boxes. Each box contains one shaped key. You need all the shapes to open the door and escape. All the information you need to solve the puzzles can be found in this book. Clues to puzzles may be on any page, so read the whole book first.

Get stuck? Answers and hints for each puzzle are found at the back of this book.

THE ELEVATORS

As you reach the end of the corridor, you see the light had been coming from two elevators. The down elevator doors are open. You see some strange objects littered around.

The up elevator's doors are locked shut. You appear to have to key in a code to open them. It's puzzling. You head into the down elevator and press the button.

THE CONTROL ROOM

The elevator doors creak shut, and it travels down, arriving in the gloomy basement. Through a doorway, you can see a bank of monitors glowing in the darkness. A mysterious box is wired to one of the monitors. You examine the screens for clues on how to get out of here. It's so creepy!

rfc lskzcp gq
rum
dmsp
cgefr

1

ACCESS DENIED!
Enter the correct code
1 2 3 4 5 6 7 8 9 0
Enter
9
OFF ON
1 1 0 0 0 1 0 1

THE RADIO ROOM

You can hear some annoying beeping coming from a narrow dark room in the basement. Peeking through the door, you see some radio equipment. The beeps seem to be coming from a pair of headphones. It looks as if someone has left in a hurry and dropped them to the floor. A large safe lies nearby.

International Morse Code

THE LONG DESK

On a long wooden desk, you find a notebook and some paper. A small safe lies on the table. Some strange symbols are drawn on the pad and the safe's keypad. A stained piece of paper is on the desk. If only you could read it properly!

Standard Code for Information
...de that turns 127 keyboard characters
...ch letter or symbol is given a number.

...alphabet start at number 65, with upper case (capital) letters
first, followed by some symbols, and then the lower case letters are
up to number 122.

Each number can then be turned into a 7-digit binary number
understood by all computers.

Type: 3

0000 1111 2222 3333

13

NOTES AND FILES

At the other end of the long desk are some scraps of squared paper. One of them has some of the squares filled in with pencil. A list of zeros and ones are next to it. Are the two connected? A small locked safe is on a nearby folder.

000010000
000111000
001010100
010010010
100010001
000010000
000010000
000010000

101110111
101000101
101000101
101110111
100010001
100010001
100010001
101110001

Zero is a number. It is halfway between -1 and 1 on a number line. Computer programmers usually start counting from zero, not one. It shows there is no amount. For example, if you have two candies and then you eat two, you have zero candies.

7 8 6 5 0
6 5
0s, then
1s, then
2s, then
3s
5 6 8 6
4 6
9 5 7 2 2 96 8 4

-3 -2 -1 0 1 2 3

BINARY

The number system we usually use is called denary.
It uses ten numbers, from 0 to 9.

0 1 2 3 4 5 6 7 8 9

Binary is a number system that only uses two numbers,
0 and 1. Programmers use binary to give commands to
computers because a computer can only understand two
states: true or false.

0 1 0 1 0 1

Programmers can use these two states to get the
computer to do things. In a drawing program, you might
program the computer to ask
"Is there a 1 assigned to a square?
If that is true, color the square in.
If that is false, leave the square blank."

1	0
0	1

TURNING BINARY INTO DENARY

To turn binary numbers into denary, you can use this chart.

8	4	2	1	denary
0	1	0	1	binary

0101 is 5

Add together numbers with a 1 underneath to work out the denary
number. This chart can give you numbers up to 15.   8+4+2+1 = 15

Each binary digit's value is twice as much as the digit to its right. Want
a bigger number? Just keep doubling the left-hand denary number and
adding it to the left until you have a big enough number!

16	8	4	2	1

32	16	8	4	2	1

SAMUEL MORSE WAS an American artist and inventor. He invented the idea of using electricity to send coded messages through wires. His electric telegraph could send and receive messages over long distances.

He created Morse Code, a system of dots and dashes that was used to spell out messages over the telegraph.

W = . _ _   A = . _   L = . _ . .   L = . _ . .

I live in a beautiful home. It is the only one on my street with a brown tiled roof. I drive to the forest most days to go for a walk. I always take my cellphone, in case there's an emergency.

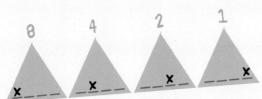

8   4   2   1

x _ _ _   x _ _ _   x _ _ _   x

start

Code scrambler

a b c d e f g h i j k l m n o p q r s t u v w x y z
y z a b c d e f g h i j k l m n o p q r s t u v w x

Set the value of x to 4

$A = x + 1$?

Set the value of x to 4

$B = x + 2$?

Set the value of x to 8

$C = x - A$?

ASCII

ASCII stands for "American Standard Code for Information Interchange." ASCII is a code that turns 127 keyboard characters into numbers. Each letter or symbol is given a number.

The alphabet starts at number 65, with uppercase (capital) letters first, followed by some symbols, and then the lowercase letters are up to number 122.

Each number can then be turned into a 7-digit binary number understood by all computers.

65 ..... A	78 ..... N	97 ..... a	110 ... n
66 ..... B	79 ..... O	98 ..... b	111 ... o
67 C	80 ..... P	99 c	112 ... p
68 ..... D	81 ..... Q	100 ... d	113 ... q
69 ..... E	82 ..... R	101 ... e	114 ... r
70 ..... F	83 ..... S	102 ... f	115 ... s
71 ..... G	84 ..... T	103 ... g	116 ... t
72 ..... H	85 ..... U	104 ... h	117 ... u
73 I	86 V	105 ... i	118 ... v
74 ..... J	87 ..... W	106 ... j	119 ... w
75 ..... K	88 X	107 ... k	120 ... x
76 L	89 ..... y	108 ... l	121 ... y
77 ..... M	90 ..... Z	109 ... m	122 ... z

BOOLEAN LOGIC

In this system of logic, two values, A and B, can each either be true (1) or false (0). Different "gates" ask different questions.

AND gates
<u>On</u>ly if A <u>and</u> B is true (1) do we get a true result (1). There are four possible answers to each question. You can record the possible answers in a truth table.

AND gate

An AND gate truth table.

A	B	output
0	0	0
0	1	0
1	0	0
1	1	1

OR gate

If A <u>or</u> B is true (1), we get a true result (1).

A	B	output
0	0	0
0	1	1
1	0	1
1	1	1

EXCLUSIVE OR gate

If A <u>or</u> B is true (1) but not <u>both</u> A and B, we get a true result (1).

A	B	output
0	0	0
0	1	1
1	0	1
1	1	0

ELECTRICAL SYMBOL GUIDE

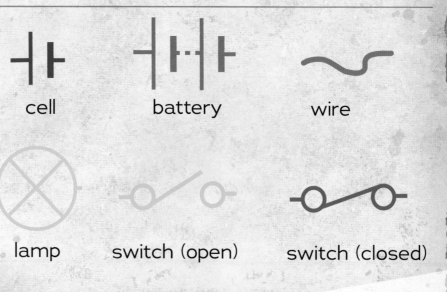

cell   battery   wire

lamp   switch (open)   switch (closed)

A cellphone communicates by radio waves using a network of base stations. The world is divided into a mosaic of small areas called "cells," each with its own base station. When a user moves from one cell to another, the phone is automatically passed to the new cell's antenna. Experts can track where someone has been by identifying the base stations that their phone used on the journey.

THE TABLET

As you turn over the folder, you find a hidden tablet and a locked box. Could the muddle of numbers on the tablet hold the key to unlocking the strange box? So many numbers! Where do you start?

THE STUDY

You search the rest of the basement for clues to help you escape. In the study area, someone has written a diagram on the blackboard. Those symbols look familiar. Perhaps you have read about them somewhere? A locked cabinet hangs on the wall.

23

THE MAP TABLE

On another table, you notice a map. A cellphone rests on a cellphone coverage map, near a locked wooden box. A red light pulses on the padlock. Maybe if you work out the cellphone passcode, you can use its remote control function and open that box.

To enable remote control, enter the passcode.

_ _ _ _ _

1 2 3
4 5 6
7 8 9
0

THE WORKBENCH

Strange tools and drawings litter the messy workbench. A locked safe is embedded in the brick wall. Symbols in the drawings seem to match symbols on the safe's keypad. That might be a clue?

SAMUEL M. WAS HERE

1

WARNING - CD Drive Error
To force eject the CD,
enter the final values
for A, B, and C.

A [ ] B [ ] C [ ]

THE STUCK CD

An open laptop is on a nearby table. You can see a broken CD stuck in the slot. The cursor on the screen is blinking. If you can crack the code, maybe you can get the CD to eject. It could be one of the keys you need to get out of here.

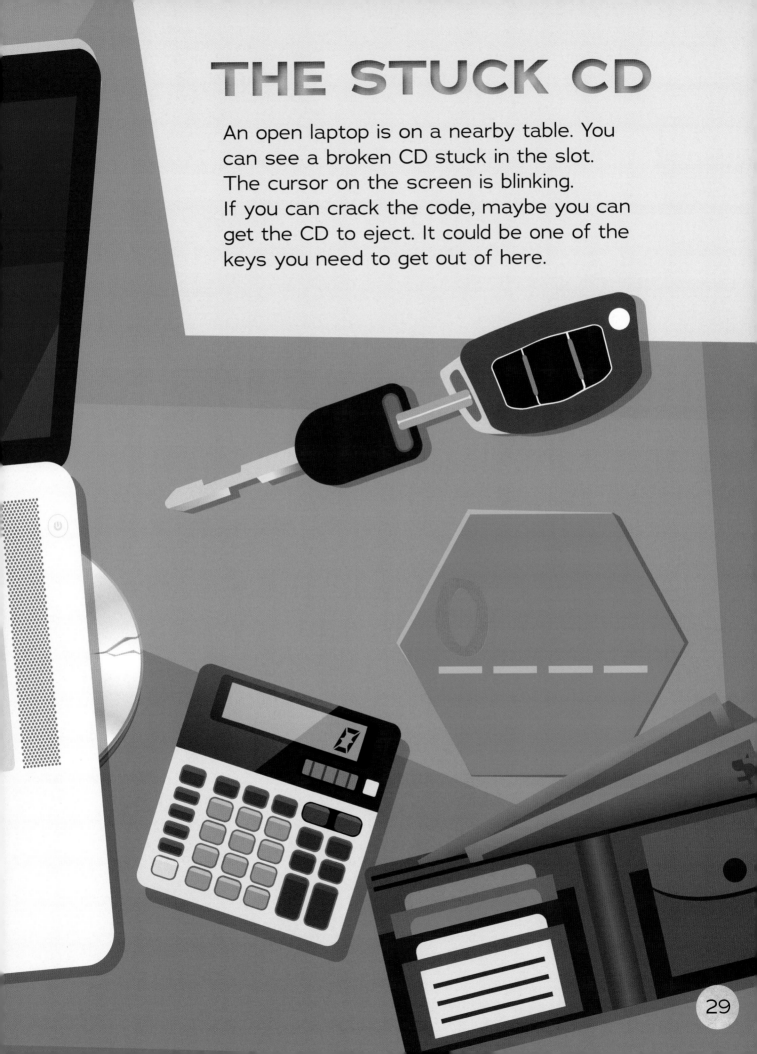

THE FILE ROOM

In the dark corner of a storeroom, a computer screen glows. The screen is covered in programming. A safe is on the desk. It needs three numbers to be entered into it. Three numbers, three pieces of programming . . . hmmm.

```
Run program 1
  start
  hold pencil
  lift pencil
  move East 1
  place pencil
  move North 1
  move North 1
  end
```

```
Run program 2
  start
  hold pencil
  place pencil
  move North 1
  move North 1
  move East 1
  move South 1
  move South 1
  move West 1
  end
```

```
Run program 3
  start
  hold pencil
  place pencil
  move East 1
  move North 1
  move West 1
  move North 1
  move East 1
  end
```

Find grid?

Did you escape the hacker's hideout?
Check your answers on page 32.

HINTS

The Elevators
1. Green shapes everywhere, and on the keypad . . .
2. Each shape has a zero or one. The order matters.
3. Write the four digits for each shape in order. The notebook shows how to turn them into numbers.

The Control Room
1. The correct code? What could that mean?
2. If only you could understand that jumble of letters on the screen.
3. The typed letters look like they might be scrambled in code.

The Radio Room
1. That poster might hold a clue.
2. The code is on another page.
3. Does it feel as if you are hitting your head on a brick wall?

The Long Desk
1. Maybe the same information on the stained note is somewhere else?
2. Find the objects to find the ASCII code.
3. Change the ASCII code into letters.

Notes and Files
1. There are the same number of binary numbers and squares on the paper.
2. The notebook may give a clue.
3. Make a grid just like the empty one on page 14. Color in all the squares where there is a 1.

The Tablet
1. A note on page 15 might help.
2. Do you have zero ideas where to start?
3. It's not the numbers; it's the patterns they make.

The Study
1. Hang each blackboard on the hook and work out the logic.
2. You need to solve A and C before you can solve B.
3. Change the number to binary using the table on the blackboard. See page 16 for help too.

The Map Table
1. Those numbers on the map might be useful.
2. Find the base stations your phone would use on your journey.
3. Check the notebook for directions.

The Workbench
1. What do those symbols mean?
2. Can you find any of the objects in the book?
3. The objects can be anywhere. Find the numbers on them.

The Stuck CD
1. A final value is the result of a sum.
2. Maybe there is a program somewhere that tells you how to find A, B, and C?
3. Do exactly what the program tells you.

The File Room
1. The programs appear to instruct you to draw something.
2. Where do you start?
3. Find a pencil, and then use the grid to draw each number.

ANSWERS
A mirror will help you read these answers.

6-7: 6392 [triangle 0110 = 6, circle 0011 = 3, square 1001 = 9, hexagon 0010 = 2]

8-9: 248 [decode the writing on the left-hand screen from the key in the notebook]

10-11: 2671 [the numbers are written in Morse code in the bricks on page 27]

12-13: ycna [the ASCII letters for the hidden numbers on the four objects]

14-15: 159 [using the grid and the binary numbers, coloring in squares with a 1 will reveal the numbers]

20-21: 1024 [Find all 0s, then 1s, 2s, and 3s. Trace their positions to form numbers]

22-23: 0635 – green A=0, B=0, C=0 [binary for 0]; red A=1, B=1, C=0 [binary for 6]; yellow A=0, B=1, C=1 [binary for 3]; blue A=1, B=0, C=1 [binary for 5] [Hang each board on the hook. Work out the Boolean logic]

24-25: 9742 [the cell base station numbers used during the journey described in the notebook]

26-27: 7639 [the numbers written on objects whose electrical diagram symbols are on the lock]

28-29: A=5, B=6, C=3 [the final values of A, B, and C from the code on page 18 of the notebook]

30-31: 105 [using the grid on page 17 follow the instructions to draw the numbers]